Little Laureates

Verses From Nottinghamshire

Edited by Mark Richardson

YoungWriters
First published in Great Britain in 2007 by:
Young Writers
Remus House
Coltsfoot Drive
Peterborough
PE2 9JX
Telephone: 01733 890066
Website: www.youngwriters.co.uk

SB ISBN 978-1 84431 254 2

Foreword

Young Writers was established in 1991 and has been passionately devoted to the promotion of reading and writing in children and young adults ever since. The quest continues today. Young Writers remains as committed to the nurturing of poetic and literary talent as ever.

This year's Young Writers competition has proven as vibrant and dynamic as ever and we are delighted to present a showcase of the best poetry from across the UK and in some cases overseas. Each poem has been selected from a wealth of *Little Laureates* entries before ultimately being published in this, our sixteenth primary school poetry series.

Once again, we have been supremely impressed by the overall quality of the entries we have received. The imagination, energy and creativity which has gone into each young writer's entry made choosing the poems a challenging and often difficult but ultimately hugely rewarding task - the general high standard of the work submitted ensured this opportunity to bring their poetry to a larger appreciative audience.

We sincerely hope you are pleased with this final collection and that you will enjoy *Little Laureates Verses From Nottinghamshire* for many years to come.

Contents

The Poems

When I Look At A Dolphin

When I look at a dolphin I can see
Her black pearly eyes staring at me.
When I look at a dolphin I can see
Her blue silky skin shining like the sea.

When I look at a dolphin I can see
Her spraying water whilst having fun with her family.
When I look at a dolphin I can see
Her pearly white teeth smiling at me.

When I look at a dolphin I can see
Her swaying fin going to and fro in the icy cold sea.
When I look at a dolphin I can see
Her whole body swaying happily.

Sasha Perkins (10)

Sounds

The spookiest sound in the world would be
An old crooked witch's bubbling tea.

The most painful sound on the Earth must be
A king cobra slithering towards me.

The happiest sound on the Earth must be
A new baby fish splashing in the sea.

The saddest sound on the Earth must be
Someone dying on the TV.

The most dramatic sound in the world will be
Somebody crying because of their knee.

The cutest sound on the Earth will be
A cat climbing up an enormous tree.

Ellie Booth (9)
Glapton Primary & Nursery School

Sounds

The spookiest sound in the world must be
A ghoul howling while chasing me.

The cutest sound in the world must be
A kitten purring at a bird in the tree.

The quietest sound in the world must be
My mum creeping down for a cup of tea.

The loudest sound in the world must be
Kathryn screaming at a bee.

Mirriam Morson (8)
Glapton Primary & Nursery School

Sounds

The loudest sound in the world must be
A volcano exploding in front of me.

The spookiest sound in the world would be
A giant jumping in front of me.

The happiest sound in the world must be
A baby laughing in front of me.

The tiniest sound in the world must be
A bee buzzing right on me.

Thomas Stocks (8)
Glapton Primary & Nursery School

Tastes

The nicest taste must be
A nice cup of tea.

The most horrible taste in the world must be
Meat on ice cream given to me.

The weirdest taste on Earth must be
Salt inside fish and meat, yucky!

The healthiest taste in the world must be
Apples growing on a tree.

Daniel Gaskell (8)
Glapton Primary & Nursery School

Sounds

The quietest sound is a little spotty ladybird eating his tea
The loudest sound is the world dropping into the beautiful blue sea
The spookiest sound in the world is zombies getting up
from their graves
The happiest sound must be a little baby laughing at me.

Kyle Stead (8)
Glapton Primary & Nursery School

Sounds

The tiniest sound in the world must be
A caterpillar eating its tea.

The spookiest sound in the world must be
A zombie growling at me.

The noisiest sound in the world must be
A volcano exploding right next to the sea.

The most miserable sound must be
Rain going down the window.

The happiest sound in the world must be
My friend cheering with me.

Thomas Lowe (8)
Glapton Primary & Nursery School

Sounds

The tiniest sound in the world must be
A centipede crawling on a branch, you see.

The loudest sound in the world must be
A giant asking for tea.

The saddest sound in the world must be
A baby crying for Mummy and me.

The noisiest sound in the world must be
An elephant stamping on me.

The happiest sound in the world must be
Me singing up a tree.

Courtney Pratt (9)
Glapton Primary & Nursery School

Lauren H (My Best Mate)

Good friend until the end
Best mate, never late
Always there, never gives me a scare
Eternal friend, right till the end.

Emma Barnett
Glapton Primary & Nursery School

What Is A Rainbow?

The rainbow is colours floating in mid-air
It is a row of coloured lines thrown in the crystal clear air
It is a splash of coloured paint all over the dull city
It is a picture drawn by a child being printed in air from Heaven
It was created by a beautiful angel, God kicked it down.

Kayleigh Mitchell (10)
Glapton Primary & Nursery School

What Is Rain?

Rain is wet, fast like a pet
It pours like a kettle
It drops like a petal
When it is in the pond
It is as bright as a magic wand.

Lucy Stocks
Glapton Primary & Nursery School

A Crocodile

Quick snapper
Water splasher
Trap maker
Death roller
Armoured creature
Flesh seeker
Carter's killer
Bone crusher.

Lee Roper
Glapton Primary & Nursery School

Tracy Beaker

Bigger shouter
Troublemaker
Heart breaker
Cake eater
Mum seeker
Fabulous fighter
Cam liker
Teacher hater
Tracy Beaker.

Katie Price
Glapton Primary & Nursery School

Summer

S unshine shining on the sea
U nder the green special tree
M unching children loving ice cream
M aking Slush Puppies just for me
E ating delicious chocolate bar
R unning out of milkshakes.

Larissa Sprake (10)
Glapton Primary & Nursery School

Summer

S un on our smiling faces
U nder wonderful places
M um and Dad having fun
M ore and more in the sun
E xciting adventure in the trees
R unning with the buzzy bees.

Molly Cresswell (9)
Glapton Primary & Nursery School

Summer Holidays

S ucking ice lollies that are cold and fruity
U nder a bright blue sky
M illions of tanned bodies all over the beach
M arvellous barbecues with tons to eat
E xciting wave fights in the sea
R ippling waves that kiss my feet

H ours of fun with my family and friends
O n the exciting Big Dipper at Blackpool
L uscious candyfloss, all sticky and sweet
I ncredible hot dogs smothered in ketchup
D azzling days that go on forever
A mazing sunsets when night-time comes
Y awns and sighs when the holiday's over
S chool uniforms ironed, another term begins.

Brandon White, Jordan Walker & Matthew Bradbury (10)
Glapton Primary & Nursery School

It's A Cave

I can hear a snake
I can feel an ache
It's a cave.

I can feel the cold
Although I'm bold
It's a cave.

I can see a light
In the dead of night
It's a cave.

I can see the walls
On which a beetle crawls
It's a cave.

I can sense freedom
To a magnificent kingdom
It's a cave.

I am starting to worry
I must hurry
It's a cave.

I can hear rocks falling
I can see my mum calling
It's a cave.

Tyler Huthwaite (10)
Glapton Primary & Nursery School

My Rabbit

My rabbit
Has fur like a travelling cloud
And is as soft as a feather pillow
That's my rabbit.

My rabbit
Is slow and sluggish like a snail
Making soft grass overturn
That's my rabbit.

But then
As fast as lightning his ears point up
He scurries home - his cage, he's safe
That's my rabbit.

Stephen Gaskell (11)
Glapton Primary & Nursery School

Horse

A grass eater
A daydreamer
A hoof clopper
A concrete scraper
A sound sleeper
A heavy eater
A rapid runner
A treat hunter
A stable keeper
A graceful jumper
A great hacker
A pandemonium causer
A placid dozer
A two-foot lander
A four-foot stander
A 13-hander . . .
A plaited beauty!

Monique Webster (11)
Glapton Primary & Nursery School

Sounds

The loudest sound in the world must be
A beating drum next to me.

The spookiest sound in the world must be
A mysterious ghost chasing after me.

The creepiest sound in the world must be
A spider catching a bumblebee.

The sweetest sound in the world must be
A baby bird cheeping just like me.

The strangest sound in the world must be
My cat purring next to me.

Alexandria Clements (8)
Glapton Primary & Nursery School

A Dragon

Air zoomer
Fire breather

Late sleeper
Giant creeper

Tail sweeper
Princess keeper

Ugly eater
Knight killer.

Aidan Frisby
Glapton Primary & Nursery School

Little Red Riding Hood

Little Red was extremely good,
She always had to wear a hood,
Delivering was her famous job,
She never paused to have a sob,
She was as sweet as cake,
Her granny loved to bake,
Laughing and playing was her game,
Little Red Riding was her *name!*

Lauren Horrey
Glapton Primary & Nursery School

What Is Grass?

The grass is a never-ending jungle
With many creatures crawling inside.

It is an emerald glimmering
As it's been pushed into the soil.

It is a seaweed-coloured sea
With endless shuddering waves.

It is a lush leaf
Covering the vast land.

The grass is a never-ending jungle
With many creatures crawling inside.

Ben Luck
Glapton Primary & Nursery School

Summer

S ea waving across the sand.
U ltimate singing in a band.
M um waving from far away.
M ama asking to play.
E xciting games to play on the sand.
R aindrops no more for a day.

Chelsea White
Glapton Primary & Nursery School

Summer Holidays

S miling kids playing in the sea
U mbrellas to buy in the fantastic shops
M oney you spend on the sweet candyfloss
M any people are buying fantastic stuff
E ating popcorn on the beach
R ides we went on were fantastic, screaming children in my ears.

H appy children on holiday
O ctopus under the sea
L ights shining on the rides
I mpressed children are just smiling
D olphins are nice and they don't bite
A nd people in rock bands rock
Y elling and screaming on the rides
S ummer holidays are my type.

Kione Bryan
Glapton Primary & Nursery School

Holidays

S ummer is the best
U nder my feet I feel the hot sand
M y boat starts to float away
M y friends rush to play
E veryone is happy in the sun
R elax and enjoy the beach.

H ot air balloons flying above the sea
O pening shops come flying through me
L ovely breeze underneath my teeth
I like to swim in the deep blue sea
D ays go past where I go last
A nd people eating ice cream
Y es, yes I'm here by my door
S ssh, it's bedtime, everyone go to sleep.

Alex King
Glapton Primary & Nursery School

Holidays

Hot as fire blazing in your eyes.
Old sand starts to fade into the ocean.
Lollies melting away.
Ice cream will have to be frozen.
Stinking dustbins overflowing,
As children play all day.
Crops soon to be harvested.
Seeds will start to germinate.

Aaron Fowler (11)
Glapton Primary & Nursery School

The Sound And Light DJ Of The Sky And Space!

I appear at night, shining the glossy and gleaming stars
Sometimes passengers come my way
I once held a disco for Neil Armstrong
His favourite song was burnished rockets blasting
When he left I gave him a souvenir of my very own cheese
If you ever want to visit me, I'm the one with the jolly face and shades
Because the sun is so bright
I once passed a radar in the sky
I think it tells the weather
When rockets pass by they're as loud as a lawnmower
revving its engine
When the sun rises high, I know it's time for my departure
So I sink down and wait for another light to shine once more!

Ellie Hickman (11)
John Hunt Junior School

Ten Things To Do With A Pencil Case

(In the style of David Orme)

Fill it full of rubbers
Paint it all sorts of colours
Hand it to a child
Make a great present
Put all your secrets in it
Hide it from everyone
Use it as a notebook
Use it as a food store
Make it sparkly, dotty or cute
Cut out little pictures.

Katie Tulett (11)
John Hunt Junior School

Lion Of The Sea

The lion is the king of the sea
His mane is scruffy and white and crashes upon the rocks
He kills the fish and he leaps on the beach
His gigantic paws are as big as lobsters
His teeth are sharp like cliff edges
He causes ultimate destruction all around
He protects boats most of the time
He sleeps through the day and plays at night
He is the king of the sea.

Joseph Noquet & Joshua Stevens (11)
John Hunt Junior School

The Sun

The sun is an evil devil
Scuttling up and down the sky
At night he hides behind the clouds
He burns humans like a thousand radiators
He controls people like a robot
Making people wear shorts and T-shirts
He kills our crops
He is a big ball of fire
He is an Earth-controller.

Joseph Parr & Hamza Javed (11)
John Hunt Junior School

The Sea Lion

I sleep in the day
I play at night
If you wake me up
Prepare to have a horrible fright
I am a colour-changing lion
That is sometimes grey and sometimes blue and green
With white powder that skims the top of my nose
If boats come near me they will be crushed with my teeth
And never underestimate the sea again
Because I am the lion of the sea!

Vikki Christian (11)
John Hunt Junior School

The Boy In The Moon

His eyes shine brightly in the night sky
His teeth sparkle in the moon's reflection
His twinkling body is as round as a ball
His mysterious glow is as bright as a torch
His breath smells like the scent of roses
He looks like a lump of white coal in the dark night sky
In the daytime he tucks his arms and legs in until the night.

Jack Dilger (11)
John Hunt Junior School

The Dark Predator

A dark figure stalks around
In the night searching for its prey
To satisfy his cruel hunger.

It uses the shadows as its ally
To protect it from many dangers
That might bring an end to it.

Then it sees its target
Two men walking down a path
It follows them to make sure they are alone.

Then it strikes, it tears out the throat
Of one of them, then the other
Just stares in horror knowing he's next.

The surviving man runs but it is much faster
It catches him, it claims its prey
For it is the Dark Predator.

Thomas Durney (11)
John Hunt Junior School

The Sophisticated Sun

I'm a mysterious golden star
I fly over flowers and make them *wilt*
I sparkle over children and make them change into lovely bouncy balls
I pounce up like a rabbit in the morning
I land like a soft squishy marshmallow at night
My wings spread out like a piece of paper floating to the ground
My eyes are like gentle and precious diamonds.

Tasmin Isaac (11)
John Hunt Junior School

The Sun

I am a space explorer
My torch lights the endless corridors of the universe
My light reaches to the very corners of the solar system
My light is all around you.

You may not be able to see me in certain parts of the day
Or if you can you don't; you're too engrossed and far away
But I'm always all around you, no matter where you are
At night I disappear but do not fear I'm always here
So no matter where you are, I'm always there
Your brightest star.

Judah Elliott (11)
John Hunt Junior School

The Golden Bird

The sun is a beautiful, bright, golden bird
The sweetest sound you've ever heard
Waiting to rise in the jewelled sky
Spreading its wings up high
Sending light down to Earth
Waiting and waiting for its birth
Scorching the dark into light
Golden feathers grow up at night
The sun is the brightest star
Play a melody with its guitar.

Maya McCree (10)
John Hunt Junior School

The Sea Lion

I sleep at day, I play at night
If you wake me out of my sleep
I'll give you a terrible fright
I'll eat your flesh if you're not careful
So beware I'm out there!

At night I roar and growl so loud
I scratch and bite the rocks, it's true
If you get in my way
I'll be after you.

Sometimes I'm green, but sometimes I'm blue
I'm suspicious you see with my changing colours
The sea creatures treat me as their queen
But remember, I can be terribly mean
My white mane skims the top of the ocean.

Soon in the summer you shall hear me miaow
Because the sun is too hot to growl so loud.

Megan Turner (10)
John Hunt Junior School

Ten Things To Do With A Pencil Case

(In the style of David Orme)

Fill it full of cornflakes to feed a hungry child
Make it into a jungle trap to catch a lion gone wild
Glam it up with jewellery, treat it like a queen
Take it everywhere with you, make it be seen
Put all your special stuff in it, make it as a spy
Then none of your stuff will go, so there's no need to cry
Keep one always spare, for an unexpected surprise
Make sure no one will see it, give it a good disguise!
Say it is your favourite thing, always feed it well
If it's been very naughty, put it in a prison cell!

Daisy Stannard (11)
John Hunt Junior School

The Dancing Sea

The sea is a dancing human
It starts off with a hula dance
It's dressed in wavy clothes, blue, green and white.

Then it does a rolling dance
It's similar to street dancing
It rolls to the sand then relaxes
Then it rolls back into the sea and gently rolls away.

Then it does a warrior dance
It's fearsome and cruel
Then the tide comes to an end
For it to start all over again.

Jessica Stapley (11)
John Hunt Junior School

The Sun Dog

The sun is just a really hot dog
A happy, barking, playing dog
He just dances and plays in the yellow warmth
And half of the day he sleeps behind a cloud
So late at night he snuggles down in the hills
The dog just lays around and relaxes
So at the end of the day
The dog just snores on the hills.

John Jessop (11)
John Hunt Junior School

Wild Wind

I am a drunk, strong boxer
I have a roaring temper
That can't be calmed down with a doctor
My hands are fierce fireballs
Wanting to burn anything in my way
I have invisible ghostly feet
That are immense
Nobody can tell who I am
I am calm one minute
And the next I am a dangerous lion.

Megan Parker (11)
John Hunt Junior School

Charlotte!

My best friend is called Charlotte
She's adventurous at climbing
But she's as quiet as a pin drop
She's as funny as a clown
But really she's as soft as a kitten
On a windy day her hair is like tangled spaghetti
She smells like a nice-smelling candle
But she loves chocolate!
My best friend Charlotte!

Emma Henfrey (11)
John Hunt Junior School

The Shark - Haiku

The shark seeks for food
His sharp teeth plunge into fish
Then he rests for night.

Lauren Cobb (11)
John Hunt Junior School

The Sea With Attitude

I am a roaring child
I crash into the rocks when I'm angry
I cry all day and night
I love to roll on the beach and splash people
I have white eyes and silver hair with long blue streaks
I have a long, flowing, light-blue dress
With lots of little fish in my hair
I'm mad and dangerous but can be a playful child
When night comes I am a soft seat for boats
With gentle snores.

Lauren Miller (11)
John Hunt Junior School

The Mysterious Moon Man

I look through the window there I see
The man in the moon looking down on me
His magical black cloak with shining sparkling stars
Unbreakable his wizard hat made by all the stars
He controls night and day with his magical moon wand
His wand is made by all the planets, one swish of it and all is done
The moon man is powerful, he is very strong
So don't blow him up with a nuclear *bomb!*

Emma Clark (11)
John Hunt Junior School

Ten Things To Do With A Pencil Case

Use it as a whack-bonk
To hit people around the head.
Fill it with water;
A hot bottle for your bed.

Use it as a lunchbox,
It keeps chocolate fresh,
Just make sure there's no pencils
Or it'll make a mess!

Use it as a sock or shoe,
(If you've lost the left or right)
Or use it as a drink holder
And fill it full of ice.

Use it as a trick or treat bag,
It'll hold candy in the night.
Give it ghostly wings and fangs
To give little kids a fright.

Just use it as a pencil case,
It's what it's built for,
Carry your pencils and your pens
For evermore.

Amy Belshaw (11)
John Hunt Junior School

I Like To Doodle!

I like to doodle
Squiggling, turning
Curling and twirling
I love to draw
Day and night
Just before tea
Beautiful portraits
Of you and me
I'd like to be famous
Roses and flowers
All at my feet
People of many
Looking for me.

Joshua O'Callaghan (10)
Langwith Bassett Primary School

Bored!

Bored is grey
Like a stormy raincloud
Hanging over you
Bored is a very dull feeling
Bored is a very unhappy feeling.

Patrick Powell (9)
Langwith Bassett Primary School

Cheetahs

Cheetahs are deadly and dangerous
They hunt their prey throughout the day
Cheetahs are yellow with black spots
But they avoid being spotted by their prey.

Cheetahs are deadly, hunting anything
Eating everything in sight
Entering in the night
Taking the chance
And eating antelope
Hoping to find help
Slithering through the grass.

Jonathon Kerr (11)
Langwith Bassett Primary School

My Brother

My baby brother is the best
Sometimes he likes to sit in his vest
He always likes to smile at me
I'll like it when he crawls
But for now he just talks
I couldn't wish for a better brother
And Jonathan is his name.

Jonathan is the best
And sometimes he wakes me up at night
He has a little blankey
And I like to squeeze him tight.

Robert Lindsley (10)
Langwith Bassett Primary School

My New Dog, Meg

Meg is a light brown
She is a chocolate fountain swirling in my mouth
She is a big, fluffy, enormous teddy bear
Meg is a warm path leading into a field full of flowers
Meg is like a sleeping baby
And also looks like one
My Meg is a really bright hot sunshine.

Sian Mitchell (10)
Langwith Bassett Primary School

The Dragon

Deep down in the dragon's lair
There are conniving, snivelling bears
Hissing vipers, biting bats
But worst of all the vicious dragon.

With eyes like fire
Skin like stone
And breath of heat and power
She's the meanest dragon you'll ever know.

She spits out deadly fire
She looks at you with might
You have every right to fear her
The dragon, the dragon, the dragon.

Leza Rossouw (10)
Langwith Bassett Primary School

Football

F ootball is the best
O pen nets are better to score
O ne goal will do
T o not draw you must try to score
B efore the match starts
A ll must train hard
L oads of fans cheer
L oads of people singing.

Steven Peake (11)
Langwith Bassett Primary School

Dragons

Dragons are big, fierce and bold
And knights come and never come back
Dragons fry knights, day and night
So they never come back
Dragons are shiny, beautiful, blue and gold
They fly day or night.

Arron Cottam (10)
Langwith Bassett Primary School

Animals

Tigers hunt like a dog eating breakfast
They don't sleep till they've eaten
They will hunt all day and hunt all night
Don't go to a tiger, you might be in sight.

Cheetahs are devastating hunters
They stalk you all night
Make sure you know where they are
They will pounce on you and you're gone.

Pandas are friendly and they're fluffy
Don't go near them
They might scratch you
So if they are above ground, stay on the floor.

Monkeys are good swingers
From tree to tree
Watch them fall down, just like me
They will climb up to swing.

James Druce (11)
Langwith Bassett Primary School

My Baby Niece

My sister Stacie,
Had a baby,
She's called Charlie,
She was born yesterday.

She sometimes has bellyache,
She gives me a headache.

She sleeps like an angel,
When she wants her bottle she cries her eyes out,
When I'm with her I soar like an angel,
When she goes out she waves her arms about,
But in the end she's my . . . baby niece.

Georgia Smith (10)
Langwith Bassett Primary School

Slavery Poem

So I am a mere chattel,
The property of my imperialist master.
Shackled in iron because of my ebony skin,
The offspring of four centuries of barbarity.
Four thousand, eight hundred months
Of unremitting toil of deprivation and degradation,
Not emancipation and education.
Reaping the Devil's legacy of death and disease.
Now, two hundred years have passed
Since William Wilberforce's Act of Abolition,
Yet, there is no apology, no shame.

Henry Appleyard (11)
Ranby House School

Apple Poem

A is for apple, round and red like the sun
P is for pineapple, like waves tumbling on rocks
P is for peach, soft and furry like a small hamster
L is for lemon, hanging like a teardrop
E is for egg plant, shiny and purple like a wizard's cloak.

Henry Isaacs (11)
Ranby House School

Fruit And Veg

A carrot is like a human,
The skin is hard and bumpy.
The inside is smooth and moist,
When you bite into it, it crunches in your mouth.

A watermelon is sweet and liquidy,
The outside looks like a meadow of lush green grass.
The inside is a rippling pink sea,
You will feel the juice watering in your mouth.

A kiwi is green and round,
Just like a bouncy ball with hair.
When cut, it's like a cricket pitch,
It melts in your mouth.

Timothy Foulds (10)
Ranby House School

Fruit And Vegetable Poem

M angos are smooth on the outside and wet on the inside
E gg plants are like giant kidney beans, purple and curled
L emons are like grapefruit, sour and round
O ranges are like the sun, round and shiny
N ectarines are like small, smooth peaches.

Oliver Bingham (11)
Ranby House School

Vegetable Cocktail

Cauliflowers and cabbages like a canopy of trees
Crunchy, crisp lettuce and bullet-like peas
Shiny black aubergines that look like my polished school shoes
Or butternut squash, which shall we use?
My favourite veggies are not those with pips,
So bring on the potatoes and make me some chips!

Oliver Jackson (11)
Ranby House School

Slave Trade

Their eyes are full of sadness,
As they sail away on ships,
In their life there is no gladness,
No nice words on their lips.

To eat, they get a small bowl of gruel,
Before they start their hard working,
This trade is immensely cruel,
With disease and illness lurking.

These people are badly treated
And I think we should call a truce,
To stop them being beaten
And cut all their chains loose.

Josephine Levick (10)
Ranby House School

The Slave Trade - What My Mother Went Through

You can see the sadness in my eyes,
The day they took my mother.
She was mistreated and injured
And they tortured her to death!

The owners were very greedy,
All they wanted was money.
The traders were racist,
They made my mother feel horrid!

This tragic moment was heartrending,
All my mother could feel was pain.
She went through so much embarrassment,
Because she was tied up in chains!

All I want is to have her back,
I want her to be by my side.
I wish this had never happened,
I wish my mother had never died!

Sophie Walker (11)
Ranby House School

Slavery

As I am in Africa, I see a man with a gun,
He puts me in chains and drags me to his ship.

I couldn't even ask why, I couldn't even say goodbye,
I tried to save my son and wife, but still they dragged them away.

I'm on his ship, I look around,
I try to comfort people, but the only thing I see, is grief.

My friend stands up, he asks a question,
Ignored, he sits back down, I would rather die than be a slave.

The man stands up and laughs out loud,
He signals to his crew to throw him overboard.

The man asks is there anyone else who wants to die?
There is absolute silence, even the cries of the babies can't
be heard.

It's now day seven, a disease has spread around,
I fear for my wife and son, as they have got the disease.

I'm now in England, my wife and son are dead,
Oh, why did this happen? I just want to go home.

Amelia Hale (11)
Ranby House School

Dreams

What are dreams? Do you know what they are?
They let you travel near and far.
In your sleep or in the day,
They let you float far away.
Daydreams are a type of dream,
They make you laugh, they make you scream.
You can have them in a car, in a house or in a bar!
You can dream about anything,
You're in control, you're the queen or king.
You rule the empire of your dreams
You may see things that you've never seen.
Nightmares are another type,
They make you shout in the night,
They make you jump, they make you scared,
They make a stir in the air.
You can dream about monsters or knights,
About castles on chocolate clouds,
About battles and famous fights
As well as silly little clowns.
My poem is nearing the end and it's time to go to sleep,
So go away and dream of things
Until another day.

Megan Clothier (11)
Ranby House School

Fruit And Veg

Fruit and veg are good for us,
Jamie Oliver tells us so.
Now let me describe some fruit and veg,
That will give you plenty of get up and go.
The inside of a kiwi is like a cricket pitch,
The outside is hairy, like a monster's foot.
The inside of a coconut, blind like fresh snow,
But eat it and you will go, go, go!
Broccoli is like summer trees,
Growing in a woodland glade.
Bananas are like canoes I row,
Yellow, smooth and curved.
The skin on a pear is like freckles,
The older it gets, the browner it becomes.
Finally . . . carrots are full of goodness,
But can I have some peas, *please*?

Beatrix Easterbrook (11)
Ranby House School

The Kumquat

Kumquat,
Round, small and juicy,
Like the core of the sun,
As yellow as a daffodil,
With its edible sweet rind
That will taste sublime
And as smooth as a fruit can be.

Matthew Bruce (11)
Ranby House School

Fruit Poem

Oranges, apples, grapes and bananas,
Just to name but a few.

Oranges, yum, round and as rough as the sun,
Orange as an orange can be,
Tasty, as an ice cream.

Apples, yum, red or green,
Great as the light of day,
Round as a ball, yet pretty as a picture.

Grapes, yum, small and sweet,
Tasty as Grandma's streamed chicken,
Red or green, it's up to you.

Bananas, yuck, crescent-shaped as the moon,
Peel off the skin to release a creamy crescent,
Ripe or not, personally I still don't like them.

James Ogley (11)
Ranby House School

World Peace

Crime and criminals,
Terrorism and racism,
Global warming and suicide bombing,
I want all these to stop.

World peace is what I wish for,
But it'll never come in my lifetime,
Only in about 1000 years,
So let's just wait and wait.

Oliver Sibson (10)
Ranby House School

She Is Emily

She is always there,
She is always so near,
She shares with me,
She invites me to tea.
We think the same things,
It's great when she sings,
She thinks it's real great,
When we stay out late,
Can't break us apart,
She is close to my heart.

Bethany Barlow (10)
Ranby House School

Millers

Martin Woods is in my box,
He loves Christmas puds,
He plays for United,
If you're thinking of Man U,
You're wrong,
He plays for Rotherham United,
The Millers they are,
The Millers they'll be,
But they are only in league three.

Thomas Horner (10)
Ranby House School

The Fox

With his big bushy tail, through my garden comes running,
He's looking for food, he's sly and he's cunning,
He's weary and witty,
Don't show him any pity,
Stand in his way and you will be history.

He kills all your chickens,
Unlike Charles Dickens who stuck to his writing,
Instead of rogue fighting,
Which seems to be this creature's favourite enlightenment,
He's full of rapid, vicious excitement.

He crosses your roads,
He snaps at your toes,
He murders your geese
And turns to cease.

He's not very pleasant,
He'd attack your pheasant,
If you gave him a chance,
To do a little prance.

He bids you adieu with blood on his lips,
He scratches his back with long fingertips,
He runs with the wind, away and away,
That was, for him, a very good day.

We've come to the end of my little rhyme,
It's really a shame we've run out of time,
Bye-bye, bye-bye, my reading friends,
Enjoy this poem to the end.

Maximillian Wilson (10)
Ranby House School

Wolf

Rabbit chaser
Sheep eater
Wild barker
Moon howler
Fast sprinter
Vicious biter
Pack hunter
Big grey wolf!

David Brown (10)
Ranby House School

Who Am I?

I am round and I am very sleepy at night
When it is bedtime I don't go to sleep
But I sleep in the day and I can roll around everywhere
I am so fast every day, mostly I roll around
I am a bit fat, but I am full of energy.

What am I?

Harriet Bennett (9)
Ranby House School

Riddle - What Am I?

I look like a fluffy ball, green and brown,
I feel as smooth as a baby,
I smell strong and taste tangy,
I have little hairs to keep me fresh,
You can find me in South Africa,
You can eat me raw or fresh,
What am I?

Calaim Parker (10)
Ranby House School

Riddle - What Am I?

I look small, mean and a tiny bit green
I feel prickly, heavy and bigger than a berry
I smell very tropical and taste it too
You can find me in a rainforest just for you!
You can eat me in a dish or on my own
What am I?

Christopher Davies (10) & Morgan Darran (9)
Ranby House School

Mmm Fruit!

Mmm fruit!
Sweet, juicy
Soft or crunchy
Crisp and tangy
Mmm fruit!

Mmm fruit!
Smooth, shiny
Rough or spiky
Hairy and downy
Mmm fruit!

Mmm fruit!
Red, green
Orange or blue
Lime and lemon
Good for you!

Zoë Kealey (9)
Ranby House School

Riddle - What Am I?

I look spiky, yellow and oval,
I feel rough, hard and heavy,
I smell fresh, tasty and juicy,
You can find me in the Caribbean,
You can eat me cold and warm,
What am I?

Jack McKay (10)
Ranby House School

What Am I?

I look long, yellow and smaller than a pineapple
I feel smooth, thin and ovalish
I smell tempting and taste lovely
You can find me in the Caribbean
You can eat me in a fruit salad and on my own
What am I?

William Walker (10)
Ranby House School

What Am I?

I look like a tennis ball
I feel like a waxed ski
I smell like a tropical rainforest
I taste like a river of juice
You can eat me with ice cream
What am I?

Adam Lowiss (10)
Ranby House School

Fruit And Veg

The green broccoli is like a woodland glade
The top of an asparagus tip is like a spear blade.

The inside of an avocado is so smooth and creamy
A pineapple's inside is so juicy, so dreamy.

A mango's inside is as sticky as a jam tart
A luscious strawberry is shaped like a heart.

A banana is shaped just like a boomerang
A lemon is sour and can make a meringue.

A cauliflower is like a tree in winter, covered in snow
An orange is like the setting sun as it glows.

A cucumber is long and green just like a snake
A coconut is so hairy and difficult to break.

Fruit and veg are so colourful and bright
To eat them is such a delight!

Isobel Clarke (11)
Ranby House School

Riddles

I look orange, scary and round
I feel rough, fat and ugly
I smell sweaty and taste horrible
You can find me on the ground
You can eat me
What am I?

I look hairy, green and ugly
I feel hairy, soft and squidgy
I smell minging and taste yucky
You can find me on the ground
You can eat me cooked
What am I?

Samuel Ablitt (10)
Ranby House School

Riddle - What Am I?

I look shiny, round and smooth
I feel waxed, squishy and light
I smell tempting and taste juicy
You can find me in Norway
You can eat me with ice cream
What am I?

Sam Humphreys (10) & Christian Smith (9)
Ranby House School

The Plantations Of Hatred

The whistling wind is biting cold,
Even in fifty degrees,
My house is a prison with bars and chains,
My wife is gone, my children dead,
I am in mercy,
My stomach is longing for hot Larna
But instead is receiving stale bread.

The plantation is the Devil's land,
The plants are grown on graves,
Their roots go down to Hell,
The sound of a whip is ever near,
As is the cruel owner,
The end is near, my future gone,
My dear reader, do please pass this on.

James Dane (10)
Ranby House School

The Phoenix

From ash I rise, from flame I'm spawned,
My wings are of fire, my eyes are like coal
And from the ash rises my soul.
As I die, I flake to ash,
But hark! I shall rise,
Look up and see me in the skies,
I am a phoenix; as ash I came and ash I will be again.

I rise again,
I fly with my kin,
To the great fire in the sky.
And I cry, 'My home, at last!'
Land and sea are nothing,
Compared to the great fire in the sky
And to it, I fly.

Daniel Parkinson (11)
Ranby House School

Little Red Riding Hood

As soon as wolf began to feel
That he would like a decent meal,
He went and knocked on Grandma's door.
When Grandma opened it, she saw,
A great claw, it knocked down the door,
It knocked her to the floor.
As the wolf came in more and more,
He slipped on the cold, wet floor.
Then he got up and went to the bed and said . . .
'Get off the floor!' then flung her out of the back door.
Little Red Riding Hood came into the house,
But she stepped on Grandma's squeaky mouse.
Then she saw the wolf and with one big whack,
The wolf's head fell into a sack.
Grandma got fed, then she went to bed.

Jack Walker (9)
St John's CE Primary School, Worksop

Food

Oh no, my chocolate is melting!
It's dripping on my hand
I'd better clean it up if I can!

My pizza is crunchy
The cheese is gooey and soft
I like it so, so much.

My marble cake is soft
It bubbles in my mouth
And tastes so gorgeous I could eat more!

Rebecca Sheldon (9)
St John's CE Primary School, Worksop

Animal Mad

A mbling alligator
B urping bison
C ool camel
D ancing deer
E ddie elephant
F ishy frog
G rumpy gorilla
H appy hyena
I gnorant iguana
J ammy Joey
K iller kangaroo
L ippy lion
M ad monkey
N asty newt
O val octopus
P iggy panda
Q ueen quail
R ampaging rhino
S harp shark
T errible tiger
U nique unicorn
V iking vulture
W impy whale
Z ippy zebra.

Thomas Renshaw (8)
St John's CE Primary School, Worksop

Alphabetical Animals

A nnoying ants
B eautiful butterfly
C ruel cats
D umb dogs
E nergetic elephants
F reaky ferrets
G iddy gorilla
H appy horse
I gnorant iguana
J umpy jaguar
K iller kangaroo
L azy lion
M ischievous monkeys
N aughty newt
O verjoyed octopus
P osh pig
Q ueen quail
R ude rabbit
S cary shark
T ense tiger
U nderweight unicorn
V icious vulture
W iggly whale
Y ummy yak
Z ipping zebra.

Elle Archer-Long (9)
St John's CE Primary School, Worksop

When Grandma Took Me Swimming

When Grandma took me swimming
Mum said, 'You be good'
But Grandma wasn't.

She pushed in the queue
And didn't pay enough
She pushed a kid
And wet the lifeguard.

She hit a lady
And hit her kids.
She stole armbands
And some goggles.

Until a lifeguard sent her out
And my grandma said,
'We'll come back as soon as we can'
I whispered, 'Next time, I'm coming with Mum!'

Lauren Bell (9)
St John's CE Primary School, Worksop

Horses

Horses run, horses walk
Horses canter on all fours
Horses have force
They run on the course
Horses can stop, horses can go
Some are fast, some are slow
Some are tall, some are small
They even go to the mall.

Elizabeth Charlie Barber (9)
St John's CE Primary School, Worksop

Gymnastics

Gymnastics is fun
But you get hot from the sun
When you do a move you are glad
But your arms and legs ache like mad.

Floor
When you do a round-off flick
After, you feel a little sick
When you present to the judge
She seems to always eat some fudge.

Bars
When you swing on bars
You feel like you're on Mars
You twirl and whirl as fast as you can
And the crowd cheers, especially that man.

Beam
When you balance on the beam
You get scared and scream
When you do the dismount
You feel glad as can be
So come and do gymnastics with me!

Charlotte Pollard (9)
St John's CE Primary School, Worksop

My Friend Luke

My friend Luke had one eye
My friend Luke bleeds all the time
My friend Luke has a mouse that is mine
My friend Luke eats pie
My friend Luke can fly
My friend Luke lives on Mars
My friend Luke eats bars
My friend Luke drives a very fast car
My friend Luke has ten wives
That is the end of my friend, Luke.

Konnor Shaw (8)
St John's CE Primary School, Worksop

Dinosaur, Dinosaur

Dinosaur, dinosaur had a big jaw
Dinosaur, dinosaur ate a big boar
Dinosaur, dinosaur went to war
Dinosaur, dinosaur gave a mighty *roar!*

Dinosaur, dinosaur eat my brother
To help save my mother
Dinosaur, dinosaur clear the lava
To help save my father.

Dinosaur, dinosaur crashed to the floor
And the door on his great big claw
Dinosaur, dinosaur ignored the law.

Hayley North (8)
St John's CE Primary School, Worksop

Mrs Delaney Is Great

She gives us loads of treats
She never shouts, 'Go to your seats!'
She has got a cat that chases mice
And she is very, very, very nice!

When I leave her class I think I'm going to cry
And she is learning how to fly
She flew to Center Parcs
Just like a skylark.

She wears a dress
I don't know if she wears a vest!

I certainly like Mrs Delaney!

Megan Reynolds (9)
St John's CE Primary School, Worksop

The Phoenix

There was a phoenix
Gliding in the air
Then he saw an enemy
So he went swooping
Down at 200mph
He brought the food back
Then got a terrible shock
His babies were gone
He went around the tree
But they weren't there
He went to the sea
And saw them dead.

Joshua Kent Garlick (8)
St John's CE Primary School, Worksop

Dinosaur Poem

Dinosaur, dinosaur went to war
Dinosaur, dinosaur gave a big roar!
Dinosaur, dinosaur has a big jaw
Dinosaur, dinosaur ate a big boar

Dinosaur, dinosaur looked at my door
Dinosaur, dinosaur crashing down my door with its claw
Dinosaur, dinosaur I got a saw
Dinosaur, dinosaur dropped to the floor.

Daniel Cashmore (9)
St John's CE Primary School, Worksop

Animal Antics

In
The
Jolly jungle
An
Ingenious iguana
Was eating a
Banana
While
A gangly giraffe
Had
A good
Laugh
Hairy hippo
Secretly loved
The
Amorous armadillo
Ant liked to destroy
Plants
While
Smelly skunk
Was sniffing
Junk
These are the world's
Craziest creatures!

Megan King (9)
St John's CE Primary School, Worksop

My Friends

My friend Little Bear
Has one ear and not much hair
His house is brown and is a lair
His teeth are sharp and ready to scare.

My friend Little Monkey
Has cool glasses and is quite funky
He wears rainbow shoes and a big gold ring
He carries a microphone and loves to sing.

My friend Army Dude
Has a pistol and is really rude
He's made of plastic and the colour green
But when threatened he is mean, mean, mean.

My friend Dinosaur
Has red skin and breaks the law
When he's mad he likes to roar
And one day he was sent to war.

My friend Slimy Snake
Likes to beat people with a rake
When he trips he likes to fake
But he always likes to break, break, break.

Alex Steeper (9)
St John's CE Primary School, Worksop

Authors

Authors are the best,
Oh where, oh where would we be without them.
When they write their books,
It helps us learn more,
Even when I read, it gives me sores.

A uthors are ace
U nbelievably fantastic
T errifically terrible
H ands hurting hourly, when they write their stories
O utstandingly perfect
R ightfully respected
S upercilious stories, so sweet, where would we be without them?

Kirsty Moody (11)
St John's CE Primary School, Worksop

My Messy Sis

My sister's room is a waste of space
She is scared of spiders so I chuck one in her face
I put aftershave in her shampoo
She smells like a pig
And she looks like one too
She hides her face behind make-up
She thinks she is cool
But she is a fool
She's got bugs in her hair
She goes up in the air
She thinks she has to shower in a dress
This is my sister, she's a big mess
But still, but still, she's the very, very best.

Agnes Toth (11)
St John's CE Primary School, Worksop

Mia, My Cat

Mia is my cat,
She isn't very fat,
My cat is lazy
And she is very crazy!

When Mia is happy,
She goes a bit wacky,
Mia sleeps on my brother's bunk bed,
Make sure she doesn't bang her head!

Mia is as thin as a twig,
Make sure she doesn't grow too big,
Just be careful, she's a devil
And you will never find her at a horse's level!

Emily Dolby (11)
St John's CE Primary School, Worksop

My Mum And Dad

My mum and dad,
Yes, they're so mean,
For they won't let me like the colour green!

My mum and dad,
Well, they're so bossy,
Cos they won't let me touch my friend's cat, Mossy!

My mum and dad,
They really are horrid,
For breakfast, I *have* to eat bowls of porridge!

My mum and dad,
I know they hate me,
Because they don't care when I hurt myself extremely!

My mum and dad,
Will they stop shouting? Will they ever?
Bet your mum and dad do this, never!

Gemma Boyd (10)
St John's CE Primary School, Worksop

Boys

Boys are mean, boys are green,
They sit on a chair, they look like a bear,
Boys are old, boys are bald.

Boys are cool, but act like a fool,
Boys are robbers, boys are joggers,
Boys are brave, boys are slaves
And boys never shave.

Girls are sweet to everyone they meet,
Girls wear pearls.

Aaron Roberts (11)
St John's CE Primary School, Worksop

Dinosaur Poem

Dinosaur, dinosaur roars so loud
Dinosaur, dinosaur is so tough
Dinosaur, dinosaur you float in the clouds
Dinosaur, dinosaur you're so rough

Dinosaur, dinosaur you've got a big jaw
Dinosaur, dinosaur have you got a big roar?

Dinosaur, dinosaur eat that boar
Dinosaur, dinosaur don't break the door
Dinosaur, dinosaur go on this tour
Dinosaur, dinosaur don't shake the floor

Dinosaur, dinosaur you've got a big jaw
Dinosaur, dinosaur have you got a big roar?

Dinosaur, dinosaur you're as fat as a boar
Dinosaur, dinosaur you've got a massive roar
Dinosaur, dinosaur don't break the law
Dinosaur, dinosaur put a plaster on that sore

Dinosaur, dinosaur you've got a big jaw
Dinosaur, dinosaur have you got a big roar?

Dinosaur, dinosaur don't you ever maul
Dinosaur, dinosaur you're meal is a boar
Dinosaur, dinosaur don't be small
Dinosaur, dinosaur don't ask for more

Dinosaur, dinosaur you've got a big jaw
Dinosaur, dinosaur have you got a big roar?

Mitchell Codd (9)
St John's CE Primary School, Worksop

Dinosaur

Dinosaur, dinosaur you have a loud roar
Dinosaur, dinosaur you broke down the door
Dinosaur, dinosaur you have a big paw
Dinosaur, dinosaur don't touch the floor

Dinosaur, dinosaur I love your big claw
Dinosaur, dinosaur doesn't it go in your paw?

Dinosaur, dinosaur fight through the war
Dinosaur, dinosaur making you fight makes you roar
Dinosaur, dinosaur go and explore
Dinosaur, dinosaur you have a scary roar

Dinosaur, dinosaur I love your big claw
Dinosaur, dinosaur doesn't it go in your paw?

Dinosaur, dinosaur your uncle is a bore
Dinosaur, dinosaur he slides on the floor
Dinosaur, dinosaur don't eat more
Dinosaur, dinosaur you have a big door

Dinosaur, dinosaur I love your big claw
Dinosaur, dinosaur doesn't it go in your paw?

Dinosaur, dinosaur what is on the floor?
Dinosaur, dinosaur who is at the door?
Dinosaur, dinosaur give him some more
Dinosaur, dinosaur was he a bore?

Dinosaur, dinosaur I love your big claw
Dinosaur, dinosaur doesn't it go in your paw?

Niamh Ankers (9)
St John's CE Primary School, Worksop

Kitten Poem

My kitten is the best
My kitten is a pest
My kitten's name is Annabel
My kitten is great.

Annabel, Annabel she is fun
Annabel, Annabel she wants a bun.

My kitten, she's got a friend
My kitten's friend lives round the bend
My kitten has a bed of gold
My kitten does me good.

Annabel, Annabel she is fun
Annabel, Annabel she wants a bun.

My kitten loves me a lot
My kitten sometimes has a cot
My kitten has a book
My kitten likes scratch poles.

Annabel, Annabel she is fun
Annabel, Annabel she wants a bun.

My kitten goes to school
My kitten is cool
My kitten does good stuff
My kitten has a good time.

Annabel, Annabel she is fun
Annabel, Annabel she wants a bun.

Lauren Atherton (9)
St John's CE Primary School, Worksop

The Poem About My Puppy

My puppy is the best
And he chews up my vest,
His name is Bean,
But to other dog's, he is very mean!

Puppy, oh puppy, are you in a hurry?
Puppy, oh puppy, don't you worry!

One day I took my puppy for a walk,
But all he would do was doggy talk,
Then I took him to the park,
But all he would do was yelp and bark.

Puppy, oh puppy, are you in a hurry?
Puppy, oh puppy, don't you worry!

When I took him back home,
He went in the garden all alone,
When I went to cheer him up,
He was talking to next door's pup!

Puppy, oh puppy, are you in a hurry?
Puppy, oh puppy, don't you worry!

He was talking in human language, that made me scared,
From that day on, next-door's puppy cared,
When I woke up the next day, he had a bag of gold,
That bag of gold looked really old.

Puppy, oh puppy, are you in a hurry?
Puppy, oh puppy, don't you worry!

Jessica Ridsdale (9)
St John's CE Primary School, Worksop

A Dinosaur Poem

Dinosaur, dinosaur you let out a big roar
Dinosaur, dinosaur you are so smart
Dinosaur, dinosaur please don't eat a wild boar
Dinosaur, dinosaur do you like the Simpson, Bart?

Dinosaur, dinosaur is so smart
Dinosaur, dinosaur please be good.

Dinosaur, dinosaur you are so tall
Dinosaur, dinosaur you are very good
Dinosaur, dinosaur you are not small
Dinosaur, dinosaur you should be good.

Dinosaur, dinosaur is so smart
Dinosaur, dinosaur please be good.

Dinosaur, dinosaur do play catch
Dinosaur, dinosaur I want to play a match
Dinosaur, dinosaur please be small
Dinosaur, dinosaur I want to play ball.

Dinosaur, dinosaur is so smart
Dinosaur, dinosaur please be good.

Connor Thackery (9)
St John's CE Primary School, Worksop

Dinosaur List Poem

Dirty dinosaur nearly dead
Dinosaur funny
Dinosaur cool
Dinosaur has got lots of money
Dinosaur wreck stuff
Dinosaur foolish
Dinosaur has got lots of fluff
Dinosaur hot
Dinosaur cool
Dinosaur watch out or you might get shot
Dinosaur good
Dinosaur bad
Dinosaur wants his pud
Dinosaur crazy
Dinosaur mad
Dinosaur watch out for the daisy
Dirty dinosaur nearly dead.

Grace Louise Elcock (9)
St John's CE Primary School, Worksop

Little Red Nose

The little red nose on the little boy's face
Was horrible and ugly, it looked a disgrace
Although he was ugly, he had an admirer
She was pretty and beautiful, her name was Kyra.

They went on boat trips, sailed the sea
Had picnics in caves
Why? Don't ask me!

They went to Spain for days and days
They went on the beach there they lay
They ate salty chips
With lovely chicken dips.

One day he went to hospital with his shiny red nose
They did operate while he had a doze
But his nose isn't red anymore, it just *grows!*

He went home, sadly with a 12-inch nose
But decided to buy Kyra a beautiful red rose
She was pleased with the rose
But dumped him for his now 15-inch long nose!

Daisy Alice Kirk (9)
St John's CE Primary School, Worksop

All The Colours

Blue is the colour of the rainbow,
Blue is the colour of the sea,
Yellow is the colour of the land,
Yellow is the colour of the sand.

Red is the colour of a poorly,
Red is the colour of a story,
Purple is the colour of a tag,
Purple is the colour of the bag.

Orange is the colour of the sun,
Orange is the colour of me having fun,
Green is the colour of the grass,
Green is the colour of the class.

Pink is the colour of a rose,
Pink is the colour of a nose,
Gold is the colour of a shoe,
Gold is the colour of dew.

Silver is the colour of a car,
Silver is the colour of a bar,
Brown is the colour of a tree,
Brown is the colour of a flea.

Megan Smith (8)
St John's CE Primary School, Worksop

My Big House

In my house there is a pig,
In my house the pig is big,
In my house in the living room there is a goat,
In my house there is a goat who has a big coat.

There's a pig that is big,
There's a horse that can do a course.

In my house there is a mouse that is small,
In my house there is a giraffe that is tall,
In my house there is a giant lion,
In my house there is a small iron.

There's a pig that is big,
There's a horse that can do a course.

In my house there is someone who is mad,
In my house that is my dad,
In my house in the bath is a dinosaur,
In my house behind the door there is a chainsaw.

There's a pig that is big,
There's a horse that can do a course.

Brandon Trolley (9)
St John's CE Primary School, Worksop

Once I Saw A Flower

Once I saw a rose,
My mum said she wanted a shot
So I did a pose
I liked it a lot.

I love flowers big and small
I love flowers short and tall.

Once I saw a buttercup
My dad wanted a photo
I was so thirsty I was holding a cup
My dad's phone said, 'Hello Moto!'

I love flowers big and small
I love flowers short and tall.

Once I saw a daisy
My sister wanted a pic
So I went to get my friend Maisy
My sister's camera went *click!*

Nichola Snape (9)
St John's CE Primary School, Worksop

Horses Around Me

My horse is a star
She is the best by far
Me and my sister give her food
We tell her off if she's rude.

Horses are great, horses are fun
They work hard to get a treat when they've done.

I love my horse
She loves me too of course
She also likes to jump
She doesn't even get a bump.

Horses are great, horses are fun
They work hard to get a treat when they've done.

Before I ride her
I brush and comb all her fur
Then I put on her tack
I don't know why but she steps back.

Horses are great, horses are fun
They work hard to get a treat when they've done.

Casey Bownes (9)
St John's CE Primary School, Worksop

I Love Chocolate

Chocolate is my dream
Chocolate and cream
I love chocolate when I am sad
I love chocolate when I've been bad
I like to sneak a bit of chocolate delight
To bring with me to a very tall height
Sometimes I like sweets
But chocolate is sweetest when I say 'eats'
Eats is my best word
When I want chocolate my mum heard
The word 'eats' attracts my mum
To give me chocolate to my tum
Chocolate is smooth when it comes to bed
I like to pretend to give chocolate to my ted
To me, chocolate is heaven
Imagine to have chocolate for eleven
I want chocolate forever
I don't want someone to ban chocolate, never!
When will I get to have chocolate with milk?
All I've had is chocolate like silk
And all I've had is chocolate that is dark
I want to take milk chocolate to the park
Because I always take dark chocolate to the park
I have a friend called Mark
Who never has chocolate that is dark
I say to my mum, it's so unfair
I want milk chocolate for a repair
I'll repair your car, honest I will
I've learnt at school, but you'll have to pay the bill
Of a tonne of milk chocolate to me
When I get it, when will it be?
I want all of the chocolate in the world
When will I get it?
This is the end of the poem about the wonderful thing
That is chocolate.

Alice Poppleton (9)
St John's CE Primary School, Worksop

Dino Rampage

Velociraptor pounce on your prey
Tyrannosaurus, tyrannosaurus, chop it today
Triceratops, triceratops, knock the rock
On the tyrannosaurus' head and knock him out.

Dino, dino, rampaging all around
Dino, dino, chomp your jaws.

Brachiosaurus, brachiosaurus, stamp your heavy feet
Shake the ground anywhere, any day
Spinosaur, spinosaur, attack gigantorsaur,
Gigantorsaur, gigantorsaur, run away from it.

Dino, dino, rampaging all around
Dino, dino, chomp your jaws.

Torosaur, torosaur, knock down the door
Smash the floor and break the back door
Kentosaur, kentosaur, you have a small jaw
And you're small than a tyrannosaur.

Kieran Cumberland (8)
St John's CE Primary School, Worksop

Red

Red is the sun
Red is the sunset
Red is some lipstick
The brick is red
And red is a football
Red is love
Red is mad.

Matthew Jones (7)
St John's CE Primary School, Worksop

I Love . . .

I love the noise of sizzling
I love the sound of drizzling
I love the smell of flowers
And the sound of birds on towers.

I love the taste of chicken legs
I love the taste of boiled eggs
I love to see my dog
But my dog hates to see me
Wearing a really wet shoe
I love to feel the wind in my face.

Reece Trolley (7)
St John's CE Primary School, Worksop

What Is Yellow?

Yellow is the fire shooting from the sun
Yellow is the sound of a big base drum
Yellow is the banana that makes a soft bite
Yellow is the sun that never said goodnight
Yellow is custard that is smooth and shiny
Yellow is small and very tiny
Yellow is butter that I like
Yellow is buttercups that I throw on a flight
Yellow is sand that is on the beach
Yellow is cheese that I like to eat
Yellow is a sweet voice that is nice and sour
Just like a lemon that I eat in an hour
Yellow is mustard that you put on a roll
Yellow is straw from a scarecrow that is stuck on a pole.

Jodie Ferrol (7)
St John's CE Primary School, Worksop

What Is Brown?

Brown is a banging noise
Brown is a tasty chocolate
Brown is a tree trunk
Brown is hot bark
Brown is gleaming eyes
Brown is hot gravy
Brown is hard bricks
Brown is dark hair
Brown is African skin
Brown can be very tired
Brown is sloppy soil
Brown is smelly onions
Brown is a box for stuff
Brown is a hard cupboard
Brown is freckles on your face
Brown is hard wood.

Ryan Hurcombe (7)
St John's CE Primary School, Worksop

The Charge Of The Fish Brigade

(Inspired by 'Charge of the Light Brigade' by Alfred, Lord Tennyson)

Half a swim, half a swim
Half a swim onward
Into seal valley
Swam the six hundred.

Forward the fish brigade,
'Ravage their whiskers!' he said,
'Capture the food,' he said
Onward they muttered.

Flippers to the right of them
Flippers to the left of them
Flippers to the front of them
Whacks unnumbered.

Crash! through the seal flanks!
Shattered their fishy tanks!
Captured the coral! Thanks
To the fish brigade!
Fishy six hundred!

Briony Rose Lawman (10)
St John's CE Primary School, Worksop

The Swarm Of The Fly Brigade

(Inspired by 'The Charge of the Light Brigade' by Alfred, Lord Tennyson)

Half a buzz, half a buzz
Half a buzz onward
Into the spider's lair
Rode the three hundred.

'Forward fly brigade!
Savage their webs!' he said,
'Capture their young!' he said
Onward they flew.

Webs to the right of them
Webs to the left of them
Webs to the front of them
Silk unnumbered.

Rip through the silky webs
Cracked their wonky legs
Captured the young! Hey
To the fly brigade!
Evil three hundred.

Sarah Gooch & Katie Martin (10)
St John's CE Primary School, Worksop

The Charge Of The Bear Brigade

(Inspired by 'The Charge of the Light Brigade' by Alfred, Lord Tennyson)

Half a growl, half a growl,
Half a growl forward,
Into sting circus,
Roared the six bears.

'Forward the bear brigade!
Ravage their honey!' he said,
'Capture their honey!' he said
Forward the bear brigade.

Stings to the right of them
Stings to the left of them
Stings everywhere, bites unnumbered.

Crash! through the bees nests!
Shattered the bees nests!
Captured the honey! Thanks
To the bear brigade
The brave six bears.

Macauley Nicholas Watkinson (10)
St John's CE Primary School, Worksop

The Charge Of The Fish Brigade

(Inspired by 'Charge of the Light Brigade' by Alfred, Lord Tennyson)

Half a length, half a length,
Half a length on,
Into shark valley,
Rode the two hundred.

'Forward the brigade!
Ravage their boat!' he said
'Capture the food!' he said
Onward they swam.

Teeth to the right of them
Teeth to the left of them
Teeth to the front of them
Swims unnumbered.

Crash! through the shark flanks
Shattered their shark food
Captured the food! Thanks
To the fish brigade!
Noble two hundred.

Steven James Gilfillan (10)
St John's CE Primary School, Worksop

Alphabet Animal

Ants are small
Ants are fast
Ants play football
Ants always come last.

Come creatures, come, I have food to give
Come creatures, come, I have food to give.

Bees are nasty
Bees are creepy
Bees eat pasties
Bees are leapy.

Come creatures, come, I have food to give
Come creatures, come, I have food to give.

Cats are so fat
Cats are so greedy
Cats sit on a mat
Cats like to be ready.

Come creatures, come, I have food to give
Come creatures, come, I have food to give
Come, come, come!

Lara Allisons (9)
St John's CE Primary School, Worksop

Yellow

Yellow is a colour
Yellow is the sun light and bright
Yellow is a sweet banana
Yellow is sand on the beach
Yellow is shiny butter
It is a pretty buttercup on a summer's day
It is fire burning wood
It is frizzy cheese
It is glamorous hair
Yellow is on a summer day
Yellow is happy
It is light
It smells like air
It tastes like lemons.

Olivia Davies (7)
St John's CE Primary School, Worksop

Golddigga

Sharp, shiny swords with glistening armour
Tremendous wings with spikes around it
Sparkling silver
Glittering gold
Hairy tail with a body so cool
Razor-sharp toes with an extraordinary yellow crown.

Joe Costello (10)
St Joseph's RC Primary School, Boughton

Dragufly

Green, big nostrils with his bushy eyebrows
Big green scales on his body
Black sharp claws on his toes and paws
Big fat belly
Teeth so sharp
Pointy spikes from head to belly.

Emma Knight (9)
St Joseph's RC Primary School, Boughton

Manalice

Five long hard legs with claws as sharp as axes
Spikes on his back and front as well
Glittering grey
Roaring red
As it came, people fled
They move craftily to catch their prey
So watch out for the monstrous thing.

Archie Banks (10)
St Joseph's RC Primary School, Boughton

Gofrat

Broad blue shoulder pads with frightening spikes
Vicious yellow teeth with bulging black eyes
Burning bronze
Nightfall-black
With cruel spikes crawling down his back
He has lanky arms and orange armour all over his face
He has padded feet with red armour covering his ears

Green, glamorous wings with a truth-telling tip
Orange helmet with a deadly spike above
Rioting red
Wicked white
This little Gofrat won't go without a fight.

Matthew Adey (10)
St Joseph's RC Primary School, Boughton

Wingus

Glistening pointed wings
With super heavyweight armour
Covered with shining silver arm pads
And has sparkling eyes

Rabbit ears
And rabbit nose
Has wrinkly feet
And pointed toes

Has muscular legs
And muscular arms
As thin as a picture frame
So he never alerts the alarms

Has a dark collar
With razor-sharp spikes
He is very popular
On the dark side

One hundred and ten miles per hour
He can run as fast as lightning
I would watch out if I were you
It may be a bit frightening.

Nathan Matthews (10)
St Joseph's RC Primary School, Boughton

Antflyninja

A helmet as black as night
Gold spikes on his red back
A pair of dark eyes and blood-red skin
Hatred running through his body
Charging at everything in sight
If attacked, he will go in flight
Golden armour covers his body
A big, heavy head with pointed antennae
Rams down every wall
Moves as quietly as a mouse.

Terrylee Robert Hunter (10)
St Joseph's RC Primary School, Boughton

Tore-Terah

Tore-Terah loves to have big spikes on his head,
In younger days, he had an army which he led.
This horrible creature lives under the sand,
Then it pops out and jumps onto the land.
It has got a snake as a tail,
We yet don't know if it's a female or male.

Tore-Terah can lurk behind every rock,
Even though it looks soft, it can pull off your sock.
Tore-Terah doesn't stay to sing,
It just flies off before you can say, 'Ping!'
Be prepared to move from house to house,
When it comes, you squeal like a mouse.

Yasmin Newton (9)
St Joseph's RC Primary School, Boughton

Peafox

Shining armour sparkling in the light,
Yellow beak as bright as the sun,
Colourful coat
Sharp spike
Magnificent tail fluttering as it flies
Long claws that scrape through skin.

Miraculous dust to make it fly,
Twisting and turning in the sky,
Like a bird catching its prey,
Swoosh!
Swoosh!
Swiftly landing on the ground,
Like a cheetah running on the plains of Africa.

Eleanor Hayward (10)
St Joseph's RC Primary School, Boughton

Crab-Wore

The terrifying creature held its helmet high,
with its right claw it nipped my thigh.
It shook off the sand,
then stretched out like a rubber band.
I backed up to the wall,
then climbed up hoping not to fall.

Ellie Goodwin (9)
St Joseph's RC Primary School, Boughton

What Is Blue?

Blue is the sky that covers the hills,
Blue is the computer room chairs in Stanhope School,
Blue is the colour of bluebells,
Blue is the colour of the background on my dad's computer,
Blue is my mum's favourite colour,
Blue is the fluffy clouds floating above me,
Blue is something that can make you feel cool,
Blue is the colour of blueberries,
Blue is a feeling that makes me happy.

Matthew Lonsdale (10)
Stanhope Primary School

Happiness - Haikus

It's all around us,
Smiling, laughing, lots of noise,
Then it slowly fades.

Smiling all day long,
Laughing about the good things,
Then in comes sadness.

Loving all good times,
Sharing all my happiness,
But sadness ends it.

Sad, unopened hearts,
Exploding dreams in my head,
Now end my sadness.

Gabrielle Jarvis (10)
Stanhope Primary School

What Is Blue?

Blue are the waves of the sea crashing on the rocks
Blue is a sapphire shining in the sun
Blue is a colour that follows us everywhere
Blue is my homework book kept in my reading folder
Blue is a Pepsi can
Blue is Manchester United's old away kit
Blue is the colour of my favourite shirt
Blue is a Lamborghini zooming on the road
Blue is the colour of the screen on my MP3 player
Blue is the crystal sky shining in my eye
Blue is the colour on my Christmas tree
Blue is the toolbar on my computer monitor
Blue is me, blue is you.

Daniel James (10)
Stanhope Primary School

Bat

Gliding in the night,
Soaring to catch some tiny prey,
Resting in the day,
Spotting some prey silently,
Kills the poor earthworm.

Cameron Stillings (10)
Stanhope Primary School

Untitled

Lion
Pounces to catch prey
Appears on Chelsea's badge
Has a big, bright mane.

Snake
Snakes slowly slither
Noiselessly over twigs
Waiting to catch mice.

Leaves
Leaves falling like snow
Flutter gently in the breeze
And silently land.

Morning
Dawn breaks, birds hatch
Birds begin to sing songs
And the world wakes to another day
Sunrise.

Liam Tarabella (9)
Stanhope Primary School

Robin

Red stomach like fire
Flying, searching for some food
Nibbling at some worms
Swallowing it with pride
Flying off again.

Sit on a rooftop
Watching as the Earth spins round
Calling to others
Then returning to its nest
Sleeping with some chicks.

Wake to a new day
Going out to look for worms
Feeding all its chicks
Going out for a quick fly
Then resting again.

Wake one more time
Slowly getting his strength back
Going for a swim
Go back for worms to eat
Calls for its bedtime.

Aaron Connelly (10)
Stanhope Primary School

Blue

Blue is the sky that I look up to every time
Blue is the sea waving about
Blue is a blueberry that you can eat
Blue are eyes that stare at me
Blue is my wallpaper that I like to see
Blue is paper that I write on
Blue is hair that I dye blue
Blue is my book that I like to read
Blue is my pen that stays in my tray
Blue is bubblegum that makes my tongue go blue
Blue is a door that I open
Blue is a lunchbox that I open to eat my dinner
Blue is a chair that I sit on
Blue is a colour of a football kit
Blue is a blueberry pie
Blue is a football
Blue is water that comes out of my tap.

Claire Johnson (9)
Stanhope Primary School

Blue

Blue is the sea so shiny and bright
Blue is you so freezing and cold
Blue is a Christmas card so nice and lovely
Blue is wallpaper so very blue
Blue is a butterfly, what a beautiful pattern
Blue is a ruler, 15 or 30cm long
Blue is yours . . . blue is mine.

Edward McCready (10)
Stanhope Primary School

Blue

Blue is the tear gathering in your sparkling eyes
When sadness comes
Blue is the salty sea causing the ocean breeze
Blue is candyfloss that likes to please
Blue is Chelsea winning the league
Blue is the sky avoiding a cloud
Blue is a primary colour that makes me proud
Blue is a strip of a rainbow leading to a pot of gold
Blue is a siren saving the old.

Jake Salmon (10)
Stanhope Primary School

Blue

Blue is the fresh feel so I can start again
And get it up to perfection
The moon is a blue mirror swimming in the sea
The strip of blue in the rainbow
I can just feel I can slide down
Blue is my bedroom that gazes at me when I go in
The moon is a blue torch guiding me home
Blue is my homework diary that I write in when I can
Blue is the sky that I want to fly through
Blue is my pen that stays in my tray
Blue is a swimming pool that I swim in most days
Blue is a rocket that is zooming off to space
Blue is my hair when I dye it blue
Blue is my bottle that I drink from every day
Blue is the shade hiding in the trees
Blue is the smell of the fresh sea
Blue is the Earth orbiting the sun
Blue is Claire's reading folder that she keeps books in
Blue is a blueberry that makes your tongue go blue.

Amber Smith (9)
Stanhope Primary School

What Is Blue?

Blue is a blueberry, a diamond glowing in the dark sky
The blue shining knight gazing in the dark dungeon
My sister's school uniform is blue like the dark blue ball
My toy dog's hair is blue like the blue waving sea
My mum mixes colour to put on hair, like the flowers in the field.

Mollie Clark (10)
Stanhope Primary School

Hayley's Blue Poem

Blue is a peacock spreading its feathers out wide
Blue is a butterfly flying in the sky.

Blue is a pencil, blue is a pen
Blue are the feathers of a hen.

Blue is fear, blue is fright
Blue is the coldness of the night.

Blue is the sea, blue is the sky
Blue is the taste of blueberry pie.

Blue is ice, blue is snow
Blue are snowdrops and freezing cold.

Blue is my bed quilt, blue is my bed
Blue is my teddy sitting on my pillow.

Hayley Douglass (10)
Stanhope Primary School

What Is Blue?

Blue is an icy cold day
Blue is when a snowman melts
Blue is when I am sad
Blue is birds flying in the air
Blue is a teardrop falling down from your face
Blue is a screen on a computer
Blue is the world falling in my hands
Blue is a paint drop splashing on my work
Blue is the sky catching my eye
Blue is the wind shooting through my ears
Blue is global warming fearing the world
Blue is the darkness of the night
Blue is the star blending with the sky
Blue is the colour of veins pumping blood through the body.

Elliot Avery (11)
Stanhope Primary School

What Is Blue?

Blue is a colour,
Blue is a car,
Blue is my brother's favourite toy.

Blue is a bus,
Blue is a chair,
Blue is my reading book.

Blue is a tear,
Blue is a mat,
Blue is *everywhere!*

Hayden Walker (11)
Stanhope Primary School

What Is Blue?

Blue is the Hulk, mighty and strong,
Blue is a fish strolling along,
Blue is my dad, very mad,
Blue is Powergen to check your meter,
Blue is a planet in the galaxy,
Blue is a tear coming from my eyes,
Blue is a blueberry squashed in my eye,
Blue is the cloud floating around me,
Blue is the sky drying my eye,
Blue is a man's colour in his eye,
Blue is a hippo jumping in the sea,
Blue is a jacket all over me,
Blue is a quiet, creepy way,
Blue is the sea, shiny and bright,
Blue is Chelsea shirt I wear for good luck,
Blue is the air floating in my eyes,
Blue is an emergency vehicle zooming to the rescue
To save the old,
Blue is my very blue hat,
Blue is a man staring in my eyes,
Blue is a man on the clouds,
Blue is Elmer's back,
Blue is a King Kong figure dropping from the sky,
Blue is the sky dropping very low,
Blue is my mum jumping up on my blue trampoline,
Blue is my dad pleading like mad,
Blue are my trainers with the Total 90 sign,
Blue is my dad looking the best man I've ever had,
Blue is my graffiti,
Blue is the colour of my Chelsea football.

Connor Stennett (9)
Stanhope Primary School

Happiness

Happiness is gold, the colour of shiny coins
Happiness is the feeling of a soft, cuddly teddy
Happiness is the smell of sweet, bright roses
Happiness is the sound of calm, slow music
Happiness is the look of a smiling, happy person
Happiness is the taste of sweet, sugary chocolate
Happiness reminds me of sweet love.

Miles Burge (8)
Stanhope Primary School

Happiness

Happiness is white like a cloud in the sky
Happiness smells like a car air freshener
Happiness looks like boats floating on a sea at night
Happiness sounds like a choir singing
Happiness reminds me of going on holiday
Happiness tastes like a chocolate bar
Happiness feels like a lavender sofa.

Lee Kendrick (9)
Stanhope Primary School

Happiness

Happiness is like a beautiful pink rose
Happiness sounds like tweeting birds in the morning
Happiness tastes like a sweet, juicy apple
Happiness smells like a bunch of yellow daffodils
Happiness looks like a colourful, bright rainbow
Happiness feels like a comfy, soft pillow
Happiness reminds me of a butterfly fluttering its beautiful wings.

Ashleigh Curwood (8)
Stanhope Primary School

Happiness

Happiness is baby-blue like the beautiful sky
Happiness sounds like an ice cream van song
Happiness tastes like crispy pancakes
Happiness smells like blossoming flowers in spring
Happiness looks like cats and dogs cute eyes
Happiness feel like a hot, warm, shower refreshing me
Happiness reminds me of my seven dogs I sold.

Chelsie Moore (8)
Stanhope Primary School

Happiness

Happiness is white like fluffy clouds
Happiness looks like a Cadbury's chocolate cake
Happiness smells like tea and shortcake
Happiness tastes like chewy toffee
Happiness sounds like the seaside
Happiness feels like a cuddly teddy
Happiness reminds me of my first ever teddy bear.

Joseph Freeman (8)
Stanhope Primary School

Happiness

Happiness is blue like the shimmering blue sky
Happiness sounds like my best friend's laughter
Happiness tastes like mouth-watering chocolate
Happiness smells like sweet-scented lavender
Happiness feels like a soft baby's bottom
Happiness reminds me of lively gymnastics.

Lauren Avery (9)
Stanhope Primary School

Happiness

Happiness is brown like my cute, fluffy cat
Happiness tastes like a scrumptious cake
Happiness smells like the sweet outdoors
Happiness feels like gooey melted chocolate
Happiness sounds like my best friend's laugh
Happiness is homework that reminds me of school.

Leah Foy (9)
Stanhope Primary School

Happiness

Happiness is silver like the twinkling stars
Happiness sounds like birds singing merrily in the trees
Happiness tastes like scones with cream all over
Happiness smells like apple crumble cooked to perfection
Happiness feels like lying down on a flowerbed
Happiness looks like a warm puppy sleeping
Happiness reminds me of lying down under the warmth of the sun.

Joe Brinley (9)
Stanhope Primary School

Happiness

Happiness is red like the Manchester United top
Happiness feels like soft sand running through your hands
Happiness looks like the beaming sun shining through the trees
Happiness smells like fish and chips at the beach
Happiness tastes like a big Galaxy chocolate bar
Happiness sounds like the ice cream van visiting my street.

Charlotte Steggles (9)
Stanhope Primary School

Happiness

Happiness is blue like the sea
Happiness feels all tickly
Happiness looks like a golden yellow flower
Happiness smells like a magnificent baked cake
Happiness sounds like my dog, Precious
Happiness tastes like a delicious marshmallow
Happiness reminds me of every episode of Doctor Who.

Louis Ingle (9)
Stanhope Primary School

Happiness

Happiness is blue like the calm, wavy sea
Happiness is like a crumbly chocolate ice cream
Happiness looks like a person having a great time at Twin Lakes
Happiness feels like my warm, fluffy scarf
Happiness sounds like a choir of tweeting birds
Happiness reminds me of old memories of my cat.

Sarah Perkins (8)
Stanhope Primary School

Happiness

Happiness is green like waving grass
Happiness looks like shimmering sugar falling from the sky
Happiness sounds like singing blue tits
Happiness feels like a juicy orange squeezing its juice
Happiness tastes like triple chocolate layer cake
Happiness smells like cookies just been made
Happiness reminds me of going on holiday.

Gabrielle Nandi (8)
Stanhope Primary School

Happiness

Happiness is purple like the scented lavender
Happiness tastes like a plump and fluffy marshmallow
Happiness feels like a mare's soft, silky mane
Happiness looks like a herd of horses running through a lush field
Happiness smells like the sweet scent of the red roses
Happiness sounds like two songbirds early in the morning
Happiness reminds me of my delightful pink bunny.

Jessica Bromhead (9)
Stanhope Primary School

Happiness

Happiness is red like a soft-petalled rose
Happiness reminds me of cute teddies
Happiness feels soft and furry
Happiness sounds like gentle music
Happiness tastes like sugary strawberries
Happiness smells like my mum's perfume
Happiness looks like the magic sun glowing on to you.

Amber Lambert (8)
Stanhope Primary School

Happiness

Happiness looks like Heaven
Happiness is like peach blossom
Happiness feels like a furry pashmina
Happiness sounds like waves splashing on a beach
Happiness tastes like gooey jam doughnuts
Happiness smells like a hot chocolate cake coming out of the oven
Happiness reminds me of white bunnies.

Ali Bordogna (8)
Stanhope Primary School

Happiness

Happiness feels like the wind blowing against my face
Happiness looks like the beach, the waves
And people on their bodyboards
Happiness smells like the freshness of the countryside
Happiness tastes like yummy chocolate caramel
Happiness sounds like waves crashing against the rocks
Happiness reminds me of the blue sea just swirling along gently.

Chloe Lineker (9)
Stanhope Primary School

Happiness

Happiness tastes like fresh, moist cake
Happiness looks like a beautiful rose
Happiness reminds me of my cuddly puppy
Happiness feels like a lovely warm bed
Happiness smells like gorgeous chocolate cake
Happiness sounds like my mum's very nice singing.

Courtney Duffield (8)
Stanhope Primary School

Happiness

Happiness is purple like one of my best friend's favourite colours
Happiness looks like children playing happily in the snow
Happiness tastes like a sweet strawberry
Happiness sounds like the laughter in a joke
Happiness reminds me of my puppy, as soft as anything.

Chloe Wood (9)
Stanhope Primary School

Happiness

Happiness is white like the floating clouds in the air.
Happiness is the smell of tulips and roses.
Happiness looks like long grass waving in the air.
Happiness reminds me of the shimmering sun in the sky.
Happiness feels like soft cotton balls.
Happiness sounds like cats miaowing.
Happiness tastes like caramel creamy chocolate bars.

Samuel Stones (9)
Stanhope Primary School

Happiness

Happiness is purple like the paint in my bedroom.
Happiness sounds like my favourite R&B song.
Happiness feels like a sunny day on the beach with your best mates.
Happiness looks like delicious Mr Whippy ice cream.
Happiness tastes like some butterscotch tart with chocolate sprinkles.
Happiness smells like warm chocolate cake,
Happiness reminds me of my family.

Chelsea Brown (9)
Stanhope Primary School

Young Writers Information

We hope you have enjoyed reading this book - and that you will continue to enjoy it in the coming years.

If you like reading and writing poetry drop us a line, or give us a call, and we'll send you a free information pack.

Alternatively if you would like to order further copies of this book or any of our other titles, then please give us a call or log onto our website at www.youngwriters.co.uk

Young Writers Information
Remus House
Coltsfoot Drive
Peterborough
PE2 9JX

(01733) 890066